AF176817

Contents

Director's foreword   Nick Mitzevich

From its inception, the national collection has been shaped by bold and ambitious acquisitions, with the aim of sharing the most significant artworks and ideas from around the world with the Australian public. One of its identifying features is the outstanding holdings of postwar American art, which remains one of the most important outside the United States. The innovation and ambition of contemporary American art is a thread that runs through the national collection, from Jackson Pollock's *Blue poles* 1952 and Andy Warhol's *Elvis* 1963, to Richard Serra's *Prop* 1968 and Eva Hesse's *Contingent* 1969, to Louise Bourgeois's *C.O.Y.O.T.E.* 1947–49 and the photographs of Diane Arbus and Cindy Sherman. The National Gallery continues to build on this legacy, with recent acquisitions including major works by Kara Walker, Nan Goldin and Matthew Barney, all of which reflect upon historical moments while resonating profoundly with the present.

Jordan Wolfson is an artist who is emblematic of the time in which we live. As we grapple with our relationship to technology, our immersion in internet culture, and with social issues of racial and gender inequality, alienation and violence, Wolfson confronts us with their images, actions and effects. His works act as witnesses on the world we are in right now, rather than taking a moral position or articulating a particular point of view. They are therefore often uncomfortable to experience, as well as being deeply intriguing in their extraordinary visual power and technical sophistication.

Body Sculpture is the third in Wolfson's series of animatronic sculptures, which have become defining works of the past decade. Each has pushed the boundaries of what we expect from a work of art, combining performance, sculpture, robotics and sound to create compelling and unsettling experiences. *Body Sculpture* takes this experience further in terms of scale, duration and complexity. Fusing abstraction and figuration, the work explores the potential of sculpture as an object in space. Its interacting robotic elements perform an intricate choreography that questions the intersection between human and machine, between embodiment and symbolism, and between object and viewer. It is the first work by Wolfson to enter an Australian collection, and we are proud to present it for the first time here in Kamberri/Canberra.

The National Gallery is privileged to have witnessed the development of *Body Sculpture* since it was commissioned in 2019. Throughout the journey we have gathered robust ideas, facilitated discussions and sought unique perspectives that position Wolfson's work within diverse contexts, including art history, cybernetics and media theory. I would like to thank the contributors to this publication, especially Jordan's close collaborator Mark Setrakian, Richard Taylor of Wētā Workshop, Russell Ferguson, a curator, writer and longtime observer of Wolfson's work, Genevieve Bell and Andrew Meares, from the Australian National University (ANU) School of Cybernetics, and artist Anne Imhof. We would also like to thank photographer David Sims and designer Joseph Logan for their creative visions in documenting and presenting the work. Finally, I thank Russell Storer for his professional diligence and commitment to this project and congratulate him on producing this exceptional publication.

We are deeply grateful to Jordan Wolfson for his ongoing commitment to this project. It is by far the most technically challenging work he has produced to date, and it has been enormously rewarding to join him on his journey over the past five years. I would also like to thank Jordan's studio team and his collaborators, who have managed the production process in Los Angeles, and the National Gallery's project team, who have contributed great expertise in realising this hugely complex production. I would also like to extend my gratitude to the artist's representatives, Sadie Coles, Larry Gagosian and David Zwirner, and to Gagosian for their production support. Thanks also go to our research partner, the ANU School of Cybernetics.

Body Sculpture is a historic acquisition for the National Gallery, marking a milestone in contemporary art. As with other great works in the national collection, it will continue to reverberate into the future.

Jordan Wolfson: *Body Sculpture*   Russell Storer

Jordan Wolfson describes his new work, *Body Sculpture* 2023, as 'figuration and minimalism meeting each other in an object'. (1) The idea came to the artist in the northern summer of 2017, while planning the third in his series of robotic installations, following *Female Figure* 2014 and *Colored Sculpture* 2016. The new work, completed after six years that included a two-year COVID-induced hiatus, has maintained its fundamental premise even as its choreography and staging has evolved dramatically through advances in programming technology and as Wolfson's intuition and ambition led it in increasingly complex directions. At the heart of *Body Sculpture* lies the fundamental question of what sculpture can be at this moment in time, when all possible materials, forms and subjects have seemingly been exhausted, and screen-based, virtual and simulated experiences dominate our social and cultural lives. In this environment of intensifying and simultaneous interconnection and atomisation, on what terms can sculpture engage us? Can objects still help us reimagine our bodies in relation to the world?

Body Sculpture extends Wolfson's longstanding exploration of form, narrative and affect into challenging and ambiguous territory. As with *Female Figure* and *Colored Sculpture*, this is a tightly structured and staged animatronic performance yet it lacks the scrutable factors those other works share. Gone are the cartoonish faces, the haiku-like voiceovers and pop-music soundtracks, components carried through from Wolfson's animated video works. Entering the gallery space, we are confronted by a large metal cube sprouting two oversized, articulated limbs and manipulated by a robotic arm using a heavy chain. These two interacting robots are framed by a giant steel gantry and sleek white platform, the proscenium stage for a performance that unfolds through a set of interlocking scenes. Over a half-hour cycle, the cube is lifted, lowered and swung around by the chain as its arms and hands enact an extraordinarily expressive range of movements from slow balletic poses to sexual or comedic gestures and frantic drumming and simulations of violence. As with all of Wolfson's works, meaning is undefined; emerging from the clashing interaction of formal elements, it finds its own way through our minds and bodies.

The choreography for *Body Sculpture* developed out of scenes that came to Wolfson as discrete 'intuitive downloads' rather than chapters in a fully plotted sequence. (2) Working with roboticist Mark Setrakian, Wolfson gradually pieced these scenes into a narrative that traverses a variety of actions, references, rhythms and emotions. The opening scene, which the artist refers to as 'sculpture garden', is slow and deliberate, comprising formal symmetrical gestures. These expressions of figuration or 'reification' establish the robotic figure as a sculpture, alert to its own historical lineages. (3) The arms and hands flow between stillness and movement, gesticulating and pausing in classical poses reminiscent of Greco-Roman, Renaissance and Hindu-Buddhist sculpture as well as modernist icons such as Constantin Brancusi's *The kiss* 1907–08. By performatively enacting its 'objecthood' in this way, the work recalls a pivotal debate in twentieth-century art in which the critic Michael Fried attacked Minimalist artists such as Robert Morris and Donald Judd for their 'literalist' incorporation of 'theatre' into the medium of sculpture by foregrounding the viewer's experience as a situation unfolding over time. (4) Judd and Morris championed a new sculptural language that employed industrial materials, highly reduced forms and methods of repetition and seriality to focus attention on the object and its presence in space. Wolfson's performing sculpture undermines the positions of both camps, breaking open Minimalism's refusal of illusionism and narrative as well as Fried's high-modernist conception of sculpture as autonomous and instantaneous, somehow existing outside of space and time.

In *Body Sculpture*'s performance, it plays most precisely off the contrast between uncannily lifelike arm and hand movements and its starkly industrial contours and infrastructure. We are obviously looking at a machine yet we feel the presence of an individual consciousness. The robotic actions become increasingly anthropomorphic as gestures shift from generic poses to specific actions, which Wolfson describes as 'this tension between personification and reification, between object and person'. (5) This dynamic is perhaps most explicit in what the artist refers to as the 'assault scene'. That scene begins slowly and sensually, the hands performing delicate gestures of self-pleasuring, caressing the 'chest' and stroking its   **7**

'head' (another uncanny aspect is how we instantly project body parts onto the work). The movements, increasingly vigorous, lead into a loud and aggressive humping of the floor. The scene reaches a climax as the arms flail around ecstatically and the hands snap into covering the 'face' in an expression of shame. The initial unfettered abandon—exploring its own physicality and surroundings, seemingly indifferent to the audience and our moral codes—shifts in a kind of Lacanian progression into a recognition as if its actions are being perceived and judged by others. (6)

Wolfson's description of this scene as 'assault' offers insight into his approach to provocative and disturbing subject matter, to present it as he sees it then leave us to draw our own conclusions. To read the scene in this light relies on assumptions and projections that lie beyond the visible: the work's gender, perhaps; the subject of the assault beyond itself and the floor; even the meaning of the term and what it applies to—could it also mean an assault on our senses and sensibilities as viewers? Encountering the scene unaware of Wolfson's terminology, we are likely to interpret it differently, yet we're being confronted not only by what we see but also by what we think we're seeing.

Body Sculpture continues Wolfson's interest in deeply conflicted human desires, particularly the latent potential for violence and how such desires are represented and received. When he references wider social issues that are at boiling points today in the United States and around the world—racism, misogyny, gender identity, white privilege, classism—they tend to be filtered through his individual characters who act out politically incorrect impulses or draw out our own, daring us to face them or to look away. The physical and spatial nature of sculpture enables Wolfson to generate a greater intensity of feeling that activates the entire body. It focuses our attention in ways that flicking through the vast assortment of online information—the contemporary condition that informs Wolfson's videos and collaged wall panels—does not. In *Colored Sculpture*, with its harrowing sequence of a Howdy Doody/Alfred E Neuman–esque mannequin swung around on a chain and smashed to the floor, its title and strung-up figure suggestive of lynching, and in the VR work *Real Violence* 2017, in which Wolfson impassively beats an animatronic white male doll with a baseball bat on a city street, strong reactions are provoked then complicated with disorienting inversions, jump cuts and ambiguities. The mannequin, for example, is a white comic-book character in brightly coloured clothing; its face switches between cute and menacing, particularly when its video-screen eyes lock onto the audience. Movements flip between gentle lowering and draping across the floor and bouts of pitiless dropping and dragging, accompanied by bursts of Percy Sledge's 'When a man loves a woman'. The soundtrack of *Real Violence* features a Hanukkah prayer, seemingly a hint at the artist's Jewish identity, although it's cut abruptly partway through, emphasising artificial relations between sound and image. As Wolfson has said of the prayer's inclusion: 'It creates a kind of poker face of absurdity to the artwork that negates meaning. They can't load meaning into it, because it. Just. Doesn't. Work'. (7)

In sidestepping meaning, Wolfson poses a challenge to this historical period when so much is at stake—a stance that has not escaped criticism. (8) As truth in politics and the media fragments and evaporates, artists are increasingly asked for moral clarity and social responsibility, with their works interpreted as evidence of their character and intentions. Wolfson's works refute these expectations: he proposes to act as witness rather than moral guide, holding a mirror up to the turbulent world around him, whether real or virtual, and inviting his audience to examine their own responses to what he shows. As he says: 'Just because you're using triggering content doesn't mean you support that triggering content. It means that you're showing it for a reason. Because it's art, and you're opening up a conversation, which is what art is supposed to do'. (9) His mashups of media imagery, internet culture and pop music with representations of sex and violence connect his work with a lineage that leads from Dada and Surrealism through Pop and on to appropriation art, Neo-Geo, the YBAs and 1990s Los Angeles artists such as Mike Kelley and Paul McCarthy. In *Female Figure*, for example, Wolfson pokes a proverbial finger

into the male gaze and its attendant anxiety through a synthesis of attraction and repulsion. The wispily clad, high-booted pole dancer with her goblin mask and basilisk stare intertwines desire and horror, reinforcing and then interrupting our process of reception in a montage of popular stereotypes and musical fragments (Lady Gaga, Paul Simon). Another part of the soundtrack includes Wolfson's voice, as if spoken by the figure, intoning 'My mother's dead, my father's dead, I'm gay', none of which are true. The mixture of confrontation and ambiguity recalls YBA artist Sarah Lucas's in-your-face *Bunny* sculptures of the late 1990s, headless sex dolls in stockings, stuffed and splayed on chairs, at once banally ordinary, grubbily funny and deeply disturbing (10), while the comic-book brutality of *Colored Sculpture* evokes McCarthy's sadistic tableaux, which also subject dolls and cartoon figures to violent actions. Both McCarthy and Wolfson explore base impulses butting up against social taboos, yet McCarthy's deranged abjection, characterised by visceral excess, contrasts with the tightly controlled and highly finished nature of Wolfson's works, with their movements clipped and constrained by a 'defined spatial volume'. (11)

Wolfson has long been interested in how to present his ideas in ways that move beyond judgement and create 'a safe space, where there appears to be no safety at all'. (12) His solution is often found through formal means with each constituent element—scale, volume, weight, duration, sound—deployed for precise effect. A key inspiration is Jeff Koons, who renders his sources from consumer culture such as advertising, bric-à-brac and commercial products as clinically detached fetish objects. Koons's works maintain their icy distance through formal enhancement: monumental scale, highly polished surfaces, high-key colours, expensive materials. His 1991 series *Made in heaven*, for instance, reframes pornographic images as glossy photos and sculptures of the artist performing elaborately staged, graphic sex acts with his then wife Cicciolina, the Hungarian-Italian porn star and politician. Wolfson cites Koons's direct gaze in these works as an important reference, providing what he calls a 'formal bridge' to the audience as if confiding 'that this is a construction that isn't intended to hurt them but to embrace them, preceded by an invitation to join him or simply watch'. (13) As Pamela M Lee writes of *Made in heaven*: 'ecstasy was less sexual than communicational, not hot, but cold … What was being communicated, finally, was the ritual of communication itself, absent questions of conflict or judgement or "middle-class" guilt over the tawdry affairs of dumb flesh'. (14)

Wolfson's formal devices also consistently remind us of their own construction. While his robotic figures fully exploit the Uncanny Valley effect in our affinity with inanimate objects, in which we feel attraction to human representations (dolls, puppets) and repulsion when they become too lifelike (automata, robots), the illusion is broken through various means. (15) In *Female Figure*, realistic skin, hair and eyes are offset by prominent mechanical joints in its shoulders and arms. The arms and hands of *Body Sculpture* look entirely robotic yet their movements appear fully human.

Among Wolfson's most distinctive 'formal bridges' is his use of sound, which intensifies affective connections with his works as well as providing unsettling counterpoints and disruptions. *Body Sculpture* brings a new turn in this: unlike his videos and two previous animatronic works, it features no recorded audio, only the noises that the robotic components make themselves. The 'drumming' scene begins with hands slapping its metal surface, beating its 'chest' in a primal expression of alpha presence and dominance. This basic 4/4 rhythm pattern is interspersed with another that is more complex, created by the fingers both separately and together. Sonically and technically, this passage is mesmerising as the intricate movements of the fingers evoke a form of ceremonial drumming. In some sequences one hand drums as the other beckons to the audience as if inviting us to join in the ritual. The passage exploits the range of tones produced across different parts of the hollow aluminium structure and by the uses of a flat palm, the side of a fist or its fingertips. To create this scene, Wolfson and Setrakian worked with the percussionist Eli Keszler to explore sonic capacities as well as the effects of different rhythms. Just after the 'assault' scene, this sequence shifts our reading of the sculpture from

being somewhat human while acting out its base animal urges back into an object, performing as a musical instrument. The scene's conclusion splits the narrative again as the robotic arm separates from and competes with the cube, grabbing and flinging the chain against one gantry tower and making its own contrapuntal beat. From a device for moving *Body Sculpture* around, the arm is now an object that seems to have an identity and motivation of its own. It consequently becomes more anthropomorphic as well—temperamental, sinuous and sinister—before returning to its support function again.

This scene expands the overall performance with the robotic arm, the chain and the gantry tower all now having active parts to play. The singular focus on the cube is broken and as the dynamic between 'object' and 'person' extends to encompass the robotic arm there is a feeling that it could potentially reach beyond the stage and turn on the audience. With the recent rapid advances of AI technology, our fear of cognisant machinery has only intensified, in particular its threats of erasing the line between reality and simulation and of replacing human functions in a kind of hostile takeover, making us redundant or even extinct. (16) Wolfson's animatronic works play on these anxieties through their uncanny simulation of human movements and emotions, although *Body Sculpture* doesn't include the face or the facial-recognition software of *Female Figure* and *Colored Sculpture*, thus lacking the direct gaze—that 'formal bridge' which Wolfson derived from Jeff Koons. For the most part the work appears blankly indifferent to the audience, its actions largely self-directed. We observe it observing itself: its physical capacity, its internal impulses and motivations, its self-realisation. The performance breaks the fourth wall at specific moments, however, such as when it beckons and points to the audience or makes cacophonous noise, disrupting the formal distance that is conventional in theatre where the spectator remains squarely outside the event.

By continually articulating and reconfiguring the relationship between performance/object and audience, Wolfson's work unsettles conventional viewing modes where we feel safely separate from the space of the artwork. The art historian Rosalind Krauss identified a similar tendency of 'attacks' on the audience within twentieth-century sculpture, which she considered 'central to the reformulation of the sculptural enterprise: what the object is, how we know it, and what it means to "know it"'. (17) These attacks include Francis Picabia's stage set for *Relâche* 1924, in which a bank of spotlights is suddenly turned on to blind the audience; Claes Oldenburg's oversized soft sculptures of everyday objects, which render them at the scale of the viewer's body; 1960s happenings in which audiences were 'assaulted' by performers, including being drenched in water, confined in tight spaces or subjected to deafening noise; and Bruce Nauman's psychologically affecting installations that use claustrophobically narrow spaces and live video feeds to 'put pressure on the viewer's notion of *himself* … as stable and unchanging in and from himself'. (18) As with Wolfson, the aim in each case has been to advance sculpture beyond traditional limits and fully engage in the present moment of encounter between the object and the embodied viewer.

Throughout *Body Sculpture*'s choreography, we are pushed and pulled, alternately seduced, distanced, fascinated and repelled. Arguably the most emotionally impactful scene comes towards the cycle's end when one hand forms the shape of a gun and acts out what appears to be suicide, pointing to itself as the other hand covers the 'face'. The sequence is performed slowly and deliberately and without apparent resolution—there is no explosive ending. In the concluding sequence, the 'face' then looks at its hands as if asking (as the artist relates) 'Who am I? What am I? What is this thing I am after I've done all of this?' (19) This scene returns to the sense of self-realisation concluding the 'assault' scene when *Body Sculpture* seems to take in the consequences of those actions and acknowledge its connection to a wider social system. It is an intriguing move in that Wolfson's works to date have been characterised by their attempts to burst through societal constraints. His push for artistic freedom echoes the Surrealist interest in disrupting the social order by releasing the subconscious in all its dreams and drives; he has cited Georges Bataille's exploration of sexual amorality in his 1928 novel *The story of the eye*

as an important inspiration. (20) It is perhaps no coincidence that a key way that the Surrealists expressed this return of the repressed was through their fascination with uncanny simulations of the human form, from dolls and mannequins to automata.

Whichever way we might experience *Body Sculpture*, Jordan Wolfson compels us to be present in that moment. He wants us to feel the full expression of conflicting sensations it provokes. His work doesn't offer answers or point the way for our responses, however much we might want it to. As his sculpture imploringly 'looks' at its hands we complete the gesture: in projecting onto this construction of moving mechanical parts we become its eyes. In this way we are also performing these actions and, perhaps, also asking questions of ourselves. Where does the machine end and the body begin?

Russell Storer is Head Curator, International Art, at the National Gallery of Australia. He has been Director (Curatorial, Research and Exhibitions) at the National Gallery Singapore, where he organised numerous exhibitions of Southeast Asian and global modern art. He has held curatorial positions at QAGOMA in Meanjin/Brisbane, where he co-curated the 6th, 7th and 8th Asia Pacific Triennials, and the Museum of Contemporary Art Australia, Gadigal Nura / Sydney, where he developed exhibitions with artists including Simryn Gill, Ugo Rondinone and Juan Davila. He was a co-curator of the 3rd Singapore Biennale in 2011 and has written widely on Asian and Australian contemporary art.

Notes

(1) Jordan Wolfson, recorded conversation with Nick Mitzevich, Los Angeles, 16 December 2022, unpublished.

(2) Wolfson with Mitzevich, 2022.

(3) See Wolfson's conversation with Anne Imhof in this publication, pp 12–17.

(4) Michael Fried, 'Art and objecthood', *Artforum*, vol 5, no 10, Summer 1967, pp 12–23.

(5) Jordan Wolfson, recorded description of *Body Sculpture*, Los Angeles, 26 May 2023, unpublished.

(6) The French psychoanalyst Jacques Lacan's theory on the stages of human psychosexual development begins with the infant phase of a pure material existence of needs and feelings; to the 'mirror stage' of recognition as 'I' through identification with one's own image; to the acquisition of language and the understanding of one's place within a social order.

(7) Jordan Wolfson in conversation with Thom Betteridge, 'How do I feel more? A weekend with Jordan Wolfson', *032C*, 24 May 2018, viewed 28 June 2023, https://032c.com/magazine/a-weekend-with-jordan-wolfson.

(8) See, for example, Rainer Diana Hamilton, 'Who likes Jordan Wolfson?', *Frieze*, 6 December 2019, viewed 28 June 2023, https://www.frieze.com/article/who-likes-jordan-wolfson.

(9) Jordan Wolfson in conversation with Anne Imhof, 'Jordan Wolfson just wants you to trust him', *Interview*, 24 October 2022, viewed 30 June 2023, https://www.interviewmagazine.com/art/jordan-wolfson-just-wants-you-to-trust-him.

(10) See, for example, Quinn Latimer, 'Describe this distance', in *Sarah Lucas: Au naturel*, exhibition catalogue, Phaidon Press, London, and New Museum, New York, 2018, p 157: '[Lucas's] sometimes humiliating treatment of the female figure might be a feminist critique of that expert level of misogyny and gender pathology in both art and life, or, conversely, a reflexive rejection of essentialist feminist readings of gender positing and positioning, but her attitude toward sexual debasement also occasionally feels more ambiguous, estranged—and disconcerting.'

(11) Mark Godfrey, 'Violence and grace: Jordan Wolfson's animatronics', in *Jordan Wolfson: manic/love/truth/love*, Rizzoli Electa, New York, 2018, p 106.

(12) Jordan Wolfson, 'Life in film (& sculpture)', *Frieze*, issue 163, 2014, p 26.

(13) Jordan Wolfson in conversation with Andrew M Goldstein, 'Jordan Wolfson on transforming the "pollution" of pop culture into art', *Artspace*, 10 April 2014, viewed 6 July 2023, https://www.artspace.com/magazine/interviews_features/qa/jordan_wolfson_interview-52204.

(14) Pamela M Lee, 'Love and basketball', in Scott Rothkopf, *Jeff Koons: a retrospective*, exhibition catalogue, Whitney Museum of American Art, New York, 2014, p 221.

(15) The roboticist Masahiro Mori's influential essay 'The uncanny valley' was first published in *Energy* in 1970. For an authorised English translation, viewed 6 July 2023, see https://spectrum.ieee.org/the-uncanny-valley.

(16) Fears of a robot takeover have been a theme in science fiction for over a century. More recently, open letters by industry leaders have been published that warn of the dangers of AI takeover. For a 2015 statement signed by Stephen Hawking and Elon Musk, among others, and a 2023 statement signed by 350 AI scientists and executives, viewed 10 July 2023, see https://futureoflife.org/open-letter/ai-open-letter/ and https://www.safe.ai/statement-on-ai-risk.

(17) Rosalind E Krauss, 'Mechanical ballets: light, motion, theater', in *Passages in modern sculpture*, Thames & Hudson, London, 1977, p 242.

(18) Krauss, p 240 (emphasis in original).

(19) Jordan Wolfson, recorded description of *Body Sculpture*, Los Angeles, 26 May 2023, unpublished.

(20) Jordan Wolfson in conversation with Stuart Jeffries, 'Jordan Wolfson: "This is real abuse—not a simulation"', *Guardian*, 3 May 2018, https://www.theguardian.com/artanddesign/2018/may/03/jordan-wolfson-puppet-violence-colored-sculpture-tate-modern.

This text has been produced from a conversation recorded in Jordan Wolfson's Los Angeles studio on 16 May 2023, with a friend, the Berlin-based artist Anne Imhof.

i.

Anne Imhof: So this is us recording a conversation [*laughs*] in Jordan's studio, looking at *Body Sculpture*.

Jordan Wolfson: Looking at *Body Sculpture* in progress.

AI: How do you make it not spin?

JW: You see that yellow gripper? It tells it [*Body Sculpture*] to just keep facing forward. It's constantly making macro or minor adjustments to keep this parallel edge of the sculpture to the parallel edge of the stage.

AI: What does that writing on the stage mean? Like, 'suicide start', 'suicide end'.

JW: So suicide is one of the things you're gonna see. That's what we're calling a symbolic vignette. One of the things the robot does, it either goes between formal and symbolic vignettes or figurative and symbolic vignettes. Suicide is one and there's one called comedy. This was all stuff we had been working on; we'd just start drawing on the stage.

AI: What was your first thought to do this piece?

JW: I had this idea of pairing minimalism to figuration. For a while I thought the piece was a little bit silly, that there was like a box with arms. But now what I understand is that it's about personification, if that's the right word, and reification, to make something like an object. So the sculpture goes between person and object or animal and object. When it does the formal movements it potentially is an object. And when it does the figurative movements it's a person.

AI: It's almost a Frankenstein version of something that's not assembled but [from which] you removed parts. You didn't give it a body or eyes, you just took them away.

JW: Yeah, I subtract.

We were talking about interactivity, how it's almost better not to be interacting, to witness it as a stranger. I think that's an intrinsic human, psychological paradigm, like seeing a public hanging or watching a trial in court or a basketball player or even an actor.

AI: There is something cruel about this too and something that makes it into a happening.

JW: The whole idea was that you experience your own body while looking at the sculpture. As I started making sculpture and looking at sculpture more actively I started realising that the sculpture was activating my body. When I was looking at it I was becoming present.

AI: I like the aspect of participation not being part of it. In my pieces it's also never participatory and I achieve this by the performers never looking at the audience.

JW: That must be very powerful, for people to be ignored by the performer.

AI: What we trained the most from the very beginning is how to look through the viewer.

These two fingers at the head [*holds up her index and middle fingers with thumb raised*] is this universal symbol for suicide. What I'm interested in, like with the suicide gesture, it's what emotion it brings and what it creates as an image. It's a gesture, you know? The thing didn't kill itself.

JW: But it gestured like the idea of killing itself.

AI: And this is what interests you with all of these movements? That they evoke something that is potentially one of the primal emotional states.

JW: Right, and here it's becoming self-aware.

AI: Yeah, it's looking at its hands.

JW: After the idea of suicide it's the idea of self-awareness. I'm not trying to moralise but after all the things it has done right here is where the last pose will go and somehow it will shut off from here.

AI: So it would be two choreographic ideas. The first would be you solve the gesture with a gesture that explains it or you add a gesture that gives another meaning to it.

JW: Yeah, I think I would rather make more meaning than make more message.

AI: There is a potency inside the gesture. Pointing to itself. And it leaves the audience to have this emotion.

JW: Exactly, the audience member either consciously or unconsciously sees themself as the proxy for the object and the object's the proxy for them.

ii.

JW: I don't want this piece to deliver a moral message about peopleness or humanness, you know, human suffering. I want the piece to be an expression of the non-dualistic unrealisedness of just being conscious and the complications and also the clarity from it. I don't want anything from the piece except for it to carry a kind of unresolved frequency.

AI: You ask yourself about consciousness [as a viewer] because it's a robot. It looks like the arm is this kind of machine and the sculpture is a sculpture but it's also a robot. And it becomes this thing in between human and machine though it's only two arms and a cube.

JW: It's quite ridiculous looking, it's absurd.

AI: Yeah, it's absurd looking. I was wondering about the name because you call it *Body Sculpture* but you actually took away the body.

JW: Like I said before it's about your body or the viewer's body.

It's an interest I have with being with objects and how an object—it sounds so simple I'm almost embarrassed to say it—can make you feel. I used to think things like video art or other types of art that used cutting-edge technology were really at the forefront. When I did *Female Figure* I realised that the presence of sculpture, the presence of an object in the space with you, is potentially the most powerful. This idea of sharing space with form and seeing yourself through form.

AI: *Female Figure* has the form of a human and you took the face away [through using] the mask, you give it hair, this amazing distortion, and it has also so much of you inside like the hand movements and your voice. Then you have *Colored Sculpture*. You use a comic style to abstract the human form. It becomes toy-like but is monstrous and has abstract arms, an abstract face. *Body Sculpture* has no eyes, no body and is just a volume, but it seems to see us and stops in front of us. It almost forces us to stand here because we believe that it's aware of our presence.

JW: What do you think of the piece?

AI: I think it's kind of a masterpiece. [*Laughs*] I've not seen something like this ever. It's not because it's robotic and this is the technique of the now. It's because I think your way of creating an art piece that evokes an emotional response in a person through feeling empathy for a thing does not match anything I've seen before.

In the choreography you set yourself in the position of the audience first, right? It's like basically experiencing the piece and making decisions. How would you describe your way of working?

JW: I think this piece was harder for me because I didn't have a lot of confidence in doing a lot of the choreography. So I kept on getting consultations from great choreographers.

AI: This is how we met.

JW: I was writing to you, How did you do that? And you're like, Oh I did that myself. And I really had to just decide.

AI: It was also the moment where you were not yet working on the choreography. It was in an in-between state.

JW: It was like this limbo state 'cause we were trapped in a kind of technical rut for about a year.

As an artist, I'm totally lost in what I'm doing. It's very confusing. I know I want to feel something but I don't know what and I'll just try everything.

AI: It's something to do with the way I think you are working and I think there's a similar way that I'm working. We have to see this stuff and through seeing things decide about what form they take. It's a method of questioning. It's not about being a genius or creating in the sense of 'mastership', but […] it's about letting things happen whether they're good or bad. I don't know how you do it with a robot.

JW: I balance out my tasks with my team's tasks. They do all the big moving parts and then we organise time for me just to play with stuff and look. I know that me looking is a lot faster than them accomplishing those big pieces. So I have to step away and it's a delicate balance.

iii.

JW: I don't mean to sound moralistic or simplistic but if one dedicates themself to something that they may have a specific aptitude for and if you get your mindset very clear, you can excel in that and it can be enormously rewarding.

AI: I often think about the aspect of talent. I think it's so important to remind myself every day that there is my talent and there's the work that I have to put into it before anything comes out of this. And that I can maintain a certain calmness and a certain focus because I would totally lose it otherwise. 'Cause I'm way too hyper and lose concentration with everyday things.

JW: I don't ever do any art or anything important unless I've meditated.

AI: So that's your practice?

JW: Yeah. And then I write in a journal. I try to write so I'm gonna do my best work and I'll be my best with the team and I'll be in my best integrity and then I write other stuff again.

AI: So it's also a wish for yourself.

JW: It's like a commitment. I think today I wrote I'm doing my best in making my most high-frequency art and with my team. And then I also write that I'm creating great wealth through sales of art and investments. [*Laughs*] I write that every day.

AI: I like that book. It's like a mantra.

JW: Yeah. So it's just about ideas, a lot of choreography ideas. This represents moving across the stage from left to right.

AI: What do you believe in when it comes to God?

JW: I believe in frequency and in consciousness. For me an artistic practice is a spiritual practice because for me to access these things I want to do I have to surrender and practise some type of spirituality to become present, to become almost this conduit or vessel for ideas.

AI: Would you say you're looking for a God in some way?

JW: No, I'm not really looking for God. I'm just looking for access. Are you looking for God?

AI: I do look for something I call God that has nothing to do with religion or my upbringing. And that something is nothing and that nothing is God. It's like an anti-god. And I think sometimes it's good to have that right in front of me. It's like your sculpture and the audience, you know? What did you call it? A proxy. The anti-god as a proxy.

JW: But I think it's not really an anti-god. I think what people don't realise is that God probably has the same intelligence level as a jellyfish and that God is just consciousness. Then you put the consciousness in a dog and you get a dog or you put the consciousness in a dolphin and you get a dolphin and you get these amazing facets of consciousness like humour and joy, even different parts like violence, hostility, neutrality, peace, restfulness.

AI: Did you work on the sculpture [so it] contains a lot of these emotions through its gestures? I want a joyful gesture,

I want sadness, I want horniness, I want aggressiveness and violence.

Or did you let Mark [Setrakian] program? And then you said, Oh, this is violent, or This gesture looks sad?

JW: I would say it's a combination of both. That's saying we're gonna create this scene that begins sensually and becomes violent. And then when Mark and I talked about the idea of pointing at itself from multiple directions, Mark took that then added the hand that moved with the trigger [gesture]. And it became immensely sad. And the slower it was the sadder it was.

Then we hired Stefan Haves; he works as a director and a consultant for Cirque du Soleil. And he came and did the comedy scene with us. I was like, I want something funny. [*Laughs*]

Looking back at it there's all the architecture of consciousness.

AI: What's the architecture of consciousness?

JW: Consciousness is like electricity. It goes into something and powers something. And then that thing is sexual or violent or funny or tender or X, Y or Z—it could be an infinite gradation of exposed emotions or whatever. I don't want to say this artwork does what people do but I guess like any artwork you'd call it like a human-condition piece or a consciousness-condition piece. But when I'm making the piece I'm lost in it, you know, I'm lost in the tunnel of it all. And I'm really trying to make decisions based on feeling and composition.

AI: To have consciousness raises a question towards artificial intelligence, towards machine-learning as a thing. This is the question now, right? Does AI have a consciousness? Can it learn to have one?

JW: I don't believe AI has a consciousness. I think probably for something to have a consciousness it requires some type of organic biological mechanism to work with consciousness. It's like a radio.

AI: Everybody's concerned to distinguish [between] human and AI. So that's in the air as a question that is almost dealt with as a currency or something.

JW: I'm not gonna comment. I think AI is gonna be very bad for privacy but it's gonna be enormously good for productivity. And of course people will lose jobs from AI. And I'm obviously not saying that's a good thing but in terms of efficiency and creating stuff with a tool it'll be enormously beneficial. For the medical industry or aeronautics industry it's gonna be great.

It would be great for me if this artwork was plugged into an AI bot; I think I could get so much done faster. I could have the ABB [robotic arm] pick up the cube and move it to that position and give us five different simulations of what it would do. Poor Ted [Marchant, lead operator] is sitting there doing that and it's taking him hours and the robot could come up with the path in five or ten minutes.

iv.

AI: Let's talk about the stage and the piece. In terms of creating a sculpture you have an object in the space and can go around it as an audience member. It has a back and it has a front so you could see it from the back but you've chosen to only give the audience access from the front. It's kind of a classical-theatre setup.

JW: You know I haven't thought about that. But when you watch how audiences look that's like a theatre setup. But you look at it like a sculpture on a pedestal, right?

AI: I love that it's like this.

JW: But just as a comparison if you looked at a Brancusi the sculpture is on a pedestal. Or if you look at Michelangelo's *David* no one can really access it from the back. I don't remember walking around it. Maybe you can but there's probably nothing to see from the back. So in a way this is the pedestal and the stage.

AI: How are you doing the scale? You have said the hands are basically oversized hands like a Renaissance sculpture. How did you measure the size?

JW: We did a bunch of versions of it and it was just about a feeling I had in my body when I looked at it at a certain scale, a certain point where it was too small and became demure or even serious then too big and it became comical. And then just right—there was just this body I would look at and a light would turn on in my body.

AI: Did you build a model for it?

JW: We had so many models and CGI models. I have a whole computer program I had built. It wasn't exactly a computer program, it was on Cinema 4D Pro where I could puppeteer the piece with all these different adjusters and levers within the program. You name it, we've done it.

AI: [*Laughs*] Did you decide from the beginning on the mechanical arm that's holding the sculpture?

JW: No. Originally it was gonna be this different one. I was showing the piece to Mike Egan who owns Ramiken Crucible, the gallery in New York City. I was talking about the problems I was having with the robotic arm. And Mike says, What does it look like unpainted? So I contact the company. I say, What does it look like unpainted? And they say, It's red with a matte, like a red primer. You could paint on top any colour: white, black, pink, whatever. And I said, Oh, interesting. Send me a picture. So he sent me a picture and I was like, It should be red but you should put a clear coat on it and make it shiny like an exposed organ, like a dog's penis or the inside of someone's mouth.

So right now it needs a little cleaning but it's shiny and almost wet-looking.

AI: It looks very powerful, like something that is pulsating and has a lot of power over the cube. Almost like a theatre play—or not theatre, it's like at a fair, something that's being shown off.

JW: Yeah, like at a carnival.

Should we keep talking?

AI: Let's stop.

JW: Let's stop.

Jordan Wolfson's *Body Sculpture* 2023 consists of a metal cube performing a series of actions over a half-hour sequence. Already in that simple sentence we are confronted with one of the work's essential elements. How can a metal cube be said to be 'performing' anything? Despite the presence of a pair of arms and hands, can we as the audience be persuaded that this object, in most ways a quintessentially inert form more associated with industrial production or minimalist sculpture, is going to perform in any way, let alone do what it eventually does, which is to engage with its observers and, indeed, elicit a series of emotional responses from them?

In a formal sense, a key progenitor of *Body Sculpture* is Tony Smith's *Die* 1962, a six-foot tube of quarter-inch hot-rolled steel. In many ways Smith's piece exemplifies the properties that we now associate with Minimalism although it somewhat precedes that movement. Weighing more than 200 kilograms and sitting directly on the floor, the sculpture seems to manifest what Martin Heidegger called *Dasein*. For Heidegger *Dasein* consisted in the most fundamental aspect of existence, preceding thought, self-consciousness and rationality. It is existence only, and '*Dasein* always understands itself in terms of its existence … The question of existence never gets straightened out except through existing itself'. (1) In *Die*, however, this absolute and apparently mute presence is surrounded by a nimbus of associations with human form and human consciousness. Smith's work was in part inspired by Leonardo da Vinci's *Vitruvian man* c 1490, a drawing of a human figure contained within a square that itself drew on the work of the ancient Roman architect Vitruvius. In the context of the Leonardo drawing then, *Die* can in some ways be thought of as a highly abstracted figurative sculpture based on human proportions. In Smith's famous exchange with Robert Morris in 1966, he explained the scale of his work in negative terms—what it was that he was not doing:

Robert Morris: 'Why didn't you make it larger so that it would loom over the observer?'

'I was not making a monument.'

RM: 'Then why didn't you make it smaller so that the observer could see over the top?'

'I was not making an object.' (2)

Smith's *via negativa* extended to the very question of whether he was making sculpture at all, preferring the ambiguous term 'presences'. As he said of his work in this vein: 'I certainly never thought of the boxes as sculpture. I just thought of them being there, which is how the word "presence" came into existence. I didn't think of them as "presences" in any melodramatic sense, but rather that I used that word simply in the context that they were there, that they were present'. (3)

It would seem then that despite its figurative references this renunciation of the melodramatic decisively separates Smith's work from Wolfson's, which is nothing if not melodramatic. Yet not quite. Smith, speaking of his cubes, quickly slid into the anthropomorphic, describing them as 'probably malignant' and said that 'they are not easily accommodated to ordinary environments, and adjustments would have to be made were they to be accepted. If not strong enough, they will simply disappear; otherwise, they will destroy what is around them, or force it to conform to their needs'. (4) The title *Die* evokes not just the cubic shape of one of a pair of dice but also, of course, death. The six-foot scale can also refer to being six feet under, as Smith acknowledged. Suddenly we seem not so far from the ambience of Wolfson's sculpture, which is quite possibly malignant and seemingly always at the point of destroying everything around it.

Although *Body Sculpture* is smaller than Smith's cube, Wolfson's work does 'loom over' the viewer since it is hoisted up on chains. We cannot walk around it since it occupies a de facto proscenium space. And it is never merely observed by the viewer. From the very beginning of our encounter with it we have the uncanny feeling that it is observing us. The cube is genderless and faceless of course, but nevertheless it is viscerally present as it moves around. It appears to have intentionality and perhaps even emotions. The most unhuman-like aspect of the cube is that it does not have a face; in particular, it does not have eyes. Yet it seems to see. It can point at the viewer.

Sigmund Freud had a long list of the elements he thought necessary for producing an uncanny effect. 'Having considered animism, magic, sorcery, the omnipotence of thoughts, unintended repetition and the castration complex, we have covered virtually all the factors that turn the frightening into the uncanny', he wrote in his highly influential essay on the subject. (5) Leaving aside Freud's persistent interest in castration, in his invocation of animism and sorcery he nevertheless identifies key elements in the uncanny. The essence of the phenomenon is that we who experience it are left in a state of uncertainty about the status of an object or persona that appears to us as recognisable, even familiar, yet at the same time deeply strange and unfamiliar.

So we face a minimalistic cube, familiar enough to anyone interested in contemporary art yet made profoundly strange because it seems to be a living entity, to have consciousness. And it has arms. It is through its arms that it manifests its consciousness. It seems that a head is not necessary for this, although it is the absence of a head that contributes to the fundamental strangeness of this object. Or would it be better to return to Smith's vocabulary and refer to *Body Sculpture* as a presence rather than an object?

The philosopher Jan Faye makes a distinction between 'representation' and 'presentation', arguing that consciousness is shaped by presentations that are directly experienced, rather than by representations, which are potentially false or at least heavily mediated, as in Plato's cave. 'A "presentation" is in some sense the real thing; a representation is a copy (often a poor one or an arbitrary stand-in for the real thing).' (6) Faye also identifies part of the difficulty we have in negotiating our relationship to objects like *Body Sculpture*. 'One reason we have so much difficulty in imagining less complex minds is that we are self-reflexive beings, consciously aware of our own imaginations and thoughts. We therefore often assume the mind to be a particular kind of unity or a substance that attentively engages itself in certain activities.' (7) In fact, one of the things that makes Wolfson's sculpture uncanny to its viewers is the sense that it might perhaps not be less complex than our own minds, that it might possibly be almost at the point of manifesting a truly self-reflexive consciousness, which would bring it disturbingly close to ourselves. At one point in the development of the work, Wolfson considered having it pull a mask in front of itself, at which point the uncanny effect would have become inescapable, with the cube showing that it was capable of hiding its appearance and identity. The ability to dissemble is all too human. It is constantly implied that the sculpture, as it comes closer and closer to achieving a consciousness of self, is approaching the point of determining its own action and of escaping altogether from the commands of its creator.

A useful point of comparison here is Wolfson's *Colored Sculpture* 2016. The similarity of the title to *Body Sculpture* already suggests this comparison, as does the fact that the figure at its centre is pulled around by chains in a cycle lasting about half an hour. In *Colored Sculpture*, however, that figure is in fully human form with a head and legs as well as arms and hands; the mechanisms of its articulation, meanwhile, are entirely visible. Above all, this figure, which resembles the puppet Howdy Doody from early American television, has eyes and they, controlled by sensors, actively make contact with audience members and follow them around the space. Even when you know how this effect works it remains deeply disturbing and uncanny. It is a genuinely frightening work and I have seen children run in terror from the space where it is displayed. But perhaps just because *Colored Sculpture* shows us a fully formed figure (in some ways a potential self-portrait of the artist), on a certain level we can deal with its upsetting and frightening qualities. Even when it is smashed into the floor we can rationalise what we are seeing at least in part because unfortunately we have all probably seen some such representation of violence inflicted on a helpless victim. 'I want people to witness themselves witnessing', Wolfson has said in describing his intentions. (8)

In the case of *Body Sculpture* the very absence of a head makes the presence stranger than the complete boy represented in *Colored Sculpture*. Yet even with no head the object is entirely readable as having some kind of consciousness. **20**

At times its arms reach under itself in a disturbingly intimate gesture. We don't quite understand the gesture and maybe we don't want to understand the gesture. At one point it mimes suicide by handgun. Sometimes its arms are extended to the sides in what inevitably suggests a crucifixion. For our sins? Wolfson definitively rejects such interpretations. 'I would really hate it if my sculpture is taken as a morality lesson', he has said. 'I'm no moralist.' (9) In this regard he is somewhat misaligned with the dominant tendencies in contemporary art, where currently much more seems invested in the idea of art as a kind of nurturing practice, ideally contributing to healing trauma.

While the caricatural view of Wolfson as a diabolical proponent of violence and abuse is clearly false, he does seem more inclined to confront and shock his audience than to comfort and reassure them. As the curator Mark Godfrey has written: 'Wolfson recognizes that our total access to every (in)conceivable image through machines and screens leads to obsessions, projections, irrational and justified fears, unfilled desires, to narcissism, to cruelty, to jealousy, and so on'. (10) It does, and Wolfson engages with all these things without feeling the need to try to assuage any anxieties such emotional responses produce.

No uplifting lesson is offered then, so don't look for one. Instead, simply allow yourself to be present and to experience the presence of this strange thing Wolfson has made, drumming on its hollow shell, pointing at you, beckoning to you.

Russell Ferguson is a curator and a writer. Formerly a curator at the Museum of Contemporary Art (MOCA), Los Angeles, the Chief Curator at the Hammer Museum, Los Angeles, and a professor at the University of California, Los Angeles, he has organised many exhibitions, including *In memory of my feelings: Frank O'Hara and American art* (MOCA, 1999); *Perfect likeness: photography and composition* (Hammer Museum, 2015); and *Bohemia: history of an idea, 1950–2000* (Kunsthalle Praha, 2023), as well as solo exhibitions by Francis Alÿs, Patty Chang, Douglas Gordon, Liz Larner, Larry Johnson and Christian Marclay. With Kerry Brougher, he also organised *Damage control: art and destruction since 1950* (Hirshhorn Museum, 2013–14).

Notes

(1) Martin Heidegger, *Being and time*, trans John Macquarrie and Edward Robinson, Blackwell, Oxford, 1962, p 33.

(2) Robert Morris, 'Notes on sculpture, part 2', *Artforum*, vol 5, no 2, 1966, p 20.

(3) Tony Smith, interview with Renee Sabatello Neu for the Museum of Modern Art, New York, 26 July 1968, archives of the Smith estate. 'Writings, interviews, letters', comp Joan Pachner, in Robert Storr, *Tony Smith*, Museum of Modern Art, New York, 1998, p 190.

(4) Tony Smith in Samuel J Wagstaff Jr, *Tony Smith: two exhibitions of sculpture*, Wadsworth Atheneum, Hartford, and Institute of Contemporary Art, Philadelphia, 1966, np.

(5) Sigmund Freud, *The uncanny*, Penguin, London, 2003, p 149.

(6) Jan Faye, *How matter becomes conscious: a naturalistic theory of the mind*, Palgrave Macmillan, Cham, Switzerland, 2019, p 5.

(7) Faye, p 33.

(8) Jordan Wolfson interview, *Judith Benhamou reports*, 30 March 2020, viewed 1 March 2023, https://www.youtube.com/watch?v=CSgG7HEBaAs&t=584s.

(9) Jordan Wolfson in conversation with Stuart Jeffries, 'Jordan Wolfson: "This is real abuse—not a simulation"', *Guardian*, 3 May 2018, https://www.theguardian.com/artanddesign/2018/may/03/jordan-wolfson-puppet-violence-colored-sculpture-tate-modern.

(10) Mark Godfrey, 'Violence and grace: Jordan Wolfson's animatronics', in *Jordan Wolfson: manic/love/truth/love*, Rizzoli Electa, New York, 2018, p 111.

This text has been produced from a series of recorded conversations that took place via Zoom on 9 and 11 March 2023 and were hosted in Te Whanganui-a-Tara/Wellington, Aotearoa/New Zealand and Los Angeles. The renowned robotics expert Mark Setrakian and his fellow special-effects pioneer Richard Taylor, creative lead at Wētā Workshop, have known each other and been industry peers for more than two decades. Setrakian has collaborated with Jordan Wolfson on all his robotic works, including *Female Figure* 2014 and *Colored Sculpture* 2016.

i.

Richard Taylor: You are putting your neck on the creative line for the audience to like or dislike what you have produced, and there is no filtration at all.

Mark Setrakian: Like with *Female Figure*: a figure standing in a space. There is flat lighting. And to your point, there is no editorial. You come in, you have full access to walk around and experience this thing as you will. Unlike Disney figures, it doesn't have the artifice of an entire environment.

RT: There is a desire to create an anti-spin and rawness between Jordan's metaphor and his analogy in his visual art. That doesn't require manipulation of the audience because he knows his audience [comprises] sophisticated, media-consuming, opinionated, politically aware, to some degree cynical citizens of the world.

MS: Developing her movements and developing the piece as a whole was highly intuitive. One of my roles is to come up with a workflow that accommodates and encourages an intuitive process where […] we don't necessarily know why we're having the emotional reaction that we have.

RT: Automata from the seventeenth and eighteenth centuries found that unique nexus point where craft and mechanics elevate into art. The thing that's mesmerising for me is the fidelity in the digits on the hands of *Female Figure*. She has no expression. But like a highly gestural news broadcaster the dexterity in her fingers is telling me what her mind is thinking.

Through the intuitive process you've treated it like a sculpture, sketching in wet clay and allowing it to imperfectly grow, ending up with these beautiful digits. Exactly like a dancer—the gestures she's doing are very much what a performer might do in front of a mirror or on a pole.

MS: I feel that hands are oftentimes more telling even than facial expression. The hands have one servo per finger and can hyperextend slightly—that hyperextension was very deliberate. One interesting thing about the *Body Sculpture* project was that Jordan wanted the hands to be able to hyperextend or transform from a left to a right, and the hands have 16 degrees of freedom. So the level of gesture is quite a bit more even than *Female Figure* is capable of.

ii.

MS: Jordan gave us a pitch video and very loosely broke down the piece into scenes. A sculpture garden. A drum scene. An assault scene. My hobby is electronic music, which has informed the design of my control system. I'm always thinking about music when I'm thinking about motion. This resonant panel [*points to panel*] was designed to act as a drumhead. It's secured along the perimeter like a drumhead, to have a wide range of tonalities [that *Body Sculpture*] could explore with its hands.

I don't think in terms of linear animation, of a storyboard, a script, a scene that comes first and a scene that comes second. I think in terms of let's make it do that thing. Let's make it do that thing twice. No, let's have it do that first thing then the third thing. Then the second thing. Actually, let's flip it around. I have this very live random-access way of going from one curated moment to another.

RT: The way a composer might sit at a keyboard. And there's no formulaic setup for the notes.

MS: Maybe you have a trusted musician and you start jamming. Basically Jordan and I are jamming. When developing 23

a scene, Jordan and I sit and talk about the moment we're trying to accomplish, the feeling we want. Then I quickly develop some material.

When you see *Body Sculpture* doing a rhythmic motion, dancing or drumming with its fingers, that cycle is part of the pose. For me, a pose is with motion. With keyframe animation instead of a pose frozen in space, that pose can have cyclical or noise-based motion built in and I can work on nuance. Then I morph into and out of it. I take that moment and stretch it, move it, rearrange it very quickly.

iii.

MS: This work is an edge case when it comes to animatronics [and] to the art world. It doesn't really have any corollary.

RT: *Body Sculpture*'s edge case is flicking back and forwards almost invisibly in that twilight hour, the blue hour between what is real, what is not, what is sentient, what is scary, what is poetic. It's able to lyrically draw a human emotion out of you because of its ability to manipulate its digits and play a visual tune for us. So it is preying on the world's paranoia about AI-driven robotics. But it is also calming because you've created something so human in its emotional interactivity with its musical self.

MS: I think it speaks to us at a very low level. A level that is a visceral, almost animal response. At the same time there is this kind of dread, a fear of the unknown.

RT: What you've created makes us feel very mortal, right down to its ability to flip its hand, right? It has achieved an anatomical dexterity that the human race has never achieved. So at one level there is wonderment. At another there is that core fear to anything we don't understand, especially when it has a threat reference in a predatorial way. You've built something that then overrides that and takes it back to its most beautiful child's-mobile-above-the-bed moment of rhythm and sound and movement.

I love that it is entirely blank and featureless. If you stay in the company of *Body Sculpture* for three minutes, five minutes, half an hour, the object is actually playing you. It's drawing out a broader spectrum of emotions than you thought you were up for when you stepped up to it.

iv.

MS: One exceptionally challenging thing [with *Body Sculpture*] was the dynamic range, from the most delicate gestures to its literally assaulting itself, the floor, pounding and lifting its weight off the ground. And the blankness, the fact that it doesn't have a face yet we can imply a face, we can imply that there's a front or a back. One exciting thing was having a character that entirely expresses itself through its hands and gross body motions, as opposed to having a facial expression or speech or anything beyond the incredible expressiveness of hands.

RT: Everyone is trying to fit the mechanics into the most refined surface area as close as possible to the human body. Here you are saying you can engender the specific emotions of the human via the ghost of the human in the shell of your robot.

MS: Jordan and I often talk about making the movement uncanny. The theory of the Uncanny Valley is that the more realistic something becomes, the more ultimately repellent it becomes. My theory is that motion is the key to circumventing the Uncanny Valley, that motion can make you empathise with a box with some arms coming out.

RT: It would be very easy just to be caught up in the wonder of it. Wow! That's incredible robotics. Poetic movement! Wow! That's a blunt and brilliant statement on the fear evoked due to the *Black mirror* robot lineage you're playing to.

MS: Jordan and I have been brutal in our editorial process in that we don't want that reaction. We want the visceral reaction, the primordial reaction, the reaction of aching in my hands when I see the gesticulations. When it starts to creep into, What a cool robot demo!—we cut that.

Something that Jordan brings up, something I think about as well, is a kind of indifference in the animal world. Certain machines are indifferent to the world. What people may think when they see it humping the floor, that's not actually our **24**

concern. Our concern is to be honest and allow it to convey that as effectively as possible.

RT: If you get down to the subtlest movement, like when you look at Tintin, the Uncanny Valley came down to whether the muscles at the corner of the mouth move like in a real mouth. How did you use motion capture? Did you get a ballet dancer in and copy their performance?

MS: There is no motion capture. Basically I create a collection of moments in poses, actions, then curate them into a timeline. But it's extremely flexible in the way it works. I want the process to be totally random. Jordan's and my creative process requires this.

Robotic anatomy is not the same as human anatomy and I want people to feel like it's human but I also want it to be hyperreal. The subtle influences of Balinese dance and of Rodin. You look at the way Rodin sculpts a hand and everything about it is fascinating, the posed fingers, the way the joints are aligned. This was one of those opportunities, and this machine can express so much with so little.

But we rebuild the creature in our minds. We see human anatomy though it's not all there. When it strikes a pose—if that pose is compelling enough—it becomes a human in our head.

v.

RT: You have a unique combination of being a roboticist and a performer, with heightened observational skills. The motor control of a ballerina or a Balinese dancer who has found control over every single muscle in every single digit and tendon of their hands, arms and bodies. Therefore it transcends physicality and becomes fantastical and magical.

MS: The sculpture-garden scene has a bit of that because *Body Sculpture* hasn't really become human yet. It's broken up into these acts and it becomes progressively more and more alive. The scene constantly challenges the viewer to perceive one facet as the front but then it becomes the back, then it becomes the top. Does it have a face or is that the chest? Or am I looking at just a box?

With these deliberate confusions you don't have to be a robotics expert to want to see a face or want to see it as anatomically related to a person. One thing we play around with is a moment where it holds a gun as if to its head and it's like, Oh, that's its head, that's its face. During the assault scene when it's rubbing its belly—well, rubbing its belly or its chest—I see that as unmistakable.

RT: What more is inside the box? What is that character thinking? How does it grow up? How does it grow old? You've created something that is not simply an object of mechanics and multi-wire interfaces. Now if something's got a personality it therefore grows, evolves, develops. I find that super exciting: it occupies space in the manner of a performance artist, in the way they form a relationship with you for a period of time. I see this character, this persona, has that, where you walk away going, I want more of that, I need to know more about that.

MS: That's a great way to think about it. I do want people to have the experience of coming and seeing *Body Sculpture* and feeling they've had an encounter and that they leave changed. Artistically it's always the goal you want, for your viewer to be a different person when they walk away.

vi.

MS: I think this piece is emerging at a very, very interesting time, both in the world of robotics and in the world of artificial intelligence.

RT: While AI robotics are commonly available in the household, they haven't been made commonly available as a performance piece. The evolution of *Female Figure* to *Body Sculpture* is a journey of trying to create things of absolute sublime beauty and performativity.

There are automata built 200 years ago that are as marvelling today as when they were built. We obviously now have an evolution of history through the awareness of automation, the coming of the motorcar, the aeroplane, the rocket ship and our cell phones, the miniaturisation of clock faces. But those automata still capture a moment of magical inspiration.

Toy technology through AI and robotics is going to be fascinating as that market competes for the space we've already seen with Robosapien of 15 years ago. That's part of *Body Sculpture* as well, the questioning of why have I now become so blasé to the reality of robotics being an integrated part of my existence?

vii.

MS: Although I am a mechanical designer the machinery and I just get drawn into the story. You and I work in the film industry and it's hard sometimes to watch a film without thinking about all the machinery that goes into filmmaking. But when it's good you're drawn in. I've really tried to accomplish that and don't want people thinking about what sort of robot it is.

There's another aspect, which is its appearance. It wears a lot of its history on its surface. We talked about different finishes for the parts, different materials for the outer cladding. I've settled on aluminium for the acoustic properties of that drumhead. That sounds so good. It's also lightweight, easy to replace if we ever have to. There are scratch marks on the arms and places where it's come into contact with itself and the floor. That all tells a story. For me the surface is not a precious surface. It's about allowing it to be a real thing and all those scratches and dings contribute.

RT: It is wearing the fatigue we would correlate to what's human in an older person. Yet it feels as if it's emerging new into life because some gestures feel like it's sensing its environment for the first time so it feels infant-like. But it's got its bruises from its confrontations. I feel that's the aspect of this character, how you've put something on the fingertip surfaces that create the thrum of sound yet those fingertips are marking and damaging the surface.

MS: Constantly, constantly changing. Many scars you see on it occurred at moments that will never come again.

RT: Although Gollum was not the first digital character committed to film his presence was the first time I felt the audience weren't arrested to say, Wow, that's a really clever use of digital effects, or That's an amazing digital character! But instead go, Gosh, there's an interesting and multifaceted performance from a movie character. I wonder whether you found that same moment here where you transcend the mechanics and the hard tech motors and linkages and the audience walk in and embrace it like they come to know a rap star or a flamenco guitarist.

MS: I feel one's first impression, depending on what it's doing when you walk into the space, is that it's unmistakably a robot.

viii.

RT: I guess one reason it's the size it is was to accommodate the mechanics of the fingers, because it all starts with the smallest motor.

MS: Jordan went back and forth about what the size is going to be. His original concept was significantly larger. But we started talking about the proportions of the arms and I finally told him, Look, I'm going to make a really great hand mechanism, I'm going to use the best servos I can. So I spent time to really develop the hand then scale the arms to that. We spent time talking about Michelangelo's *David* and made the hands on the large side. In some ways the most important element, the hands, guided the creation of the entire piece.

It's very much an edge case in almost every way. The materials are being pushed to the edge. The motors are pushed to the edge of their speed and torque. Everything about it is challenging.

RT: What you've extrapolated is the ability to create muscular control in individual joints, which is bonkers. Then you have the great advantage that it can reverse-perform in the hand, which brings the surreal to the sublime, which is very spooky. **26**

MS: As a viewer, you look at it and say, Oh yeah, there's a hand. Then when it flips, it's shocking because you didn't see it coming.

RT: In the performance, are you going to lull people into a false sense of security by a hand giving a humanoid performance for a time and only then flip it?

MS: It's entirely indifferent. It organically fits into the choreography. There's a moment in the drum scene where the hand is dancing and sort of hyperextends. It goes from being entirely figurative then in an instant suddenly it becomes abstract.

That goes for all the choreography, really. When we get to the point where it doesn't seem calculated, it feels very organic. That's when we know it's right. That's another aspect to having a tool set that allows for an improvisational approach to developing the animation.

It was very important to me, and this goes back to *Female Figure*, to not have a linear system where we have a beginning, a middle and an end and we always know where we're working. I wanted a system where we could work on a moment and could work on another moment and could put them together or change them or stretch them out so these moments coalesce into a performance then coalesce into the piece. And as we develop the material, we can then decide what the beginning and middle and end is.

But with the freedom to make discoveries along the way, to have accidents and intuitions. And then pursue those without having to say, Oh well, let's splice something in the middle of this. It really doesn't have to work that way. It's entirely fluid and sculptural.

And the way that plays into the work that we're doing in choreography is that it gives us the freedom to follow where it leads. You know, as if there's no plan. I did this a few nights ago. I wanted to develop a scene and did the first motions of the scene and allowed myself to be drawn in. Pretty soon I had a five-minute scene, which is frankly too long. But it took me somewhere and the tools allowed me to follow in this improvisational way.

RT: What you and Jordan have built and your control system that people won't even get to see is the transition on from the Boston Dynamics robot doing its wonderful backflips. That robot does not have the ability to improvise that I can see, and apologies to the Boston Dynamics people if they have done that. But over the times I've caught up with you, the things you've shown me aspire to elevate above mechanical input, driving motors via signals, and provide the fluidity to intellectualise and choreograph improvisation. This work is trying to ensure that the ghost and the machine have improvisational fluidity, so following where it leads.

ix.

MS: There are two areas where I'm constantly working. One is, What technical problem do I have to solve today? What barrier do I have to overcome to get this thing to move on to the next stage? About the thumb, this has a very interesting thumb-folding mechanism. What's funny is that the hand is of course symmetrical right down this plane [*traces the spot*]. So already it's a compromise that it's symmetrical in this central plane. But it works. It comes around.

Is it innovative? I'm not sure it was. It was the solution I had to come up with to make this work over and over again. That's what I've been doing: come up with a solution that leads to a compelling performance.

What innovation am I going to come up with today? I never think that. I think, How much better can this get? Sometimes it's writing a new feature into the software. The one I'm working on at the moment is so when it's hanging from the chain it can actually impart motion. It can start rocking around. Then the question becomes, Well, if I can start the rocking, can I stop the rocking? Can I invert that force and make it freeze in space? Well, let's see if I can get that done.

It's the thing I have to do to make this work the way I want it to work. That's been the nature of my career. Working **27**

on Stuntronic Spider-man was interesting because at Disney they're very cognisant of the degree to which they're innovating. They are also patenting what they work on. I knew what I wanted to do, I knew how to get to the finish line. Along the way it was like, Okay, is this an innovation?

RT: At home at night going, Oh, if I dismantle this motor and put this thing on the back of it I might go back to the manufacturer and get royalties.

MS: You just touched on something which is the core of classic creature effects: that we're constantly using things that were meant for something else. We're constantly capitalising on technologies not intended for what we're using them for. If the company that manufactures the servos I use saw a scene of this [object] pounding itself and picking itself up off the ground they would probably turn ashen and say, Oh my God, there must be following errors.

Yeah, there's following errors, it's throwing following errors all the time. But it works. That idea of taking something and pushing it outside its original-use case.

At every stage of technique since Daedalus or Hero of Alexandria, the ability of the artificer to produce a working simulacrum of a living organism has always intrigued people. This desire to produce and to study automata has always been expressed in terms of the living technique of the age. (1)

Norbert Wiener

Jordan Wolfson's unsettling experiments with automata have a long and complicating pre/history.

For more than a thousand years, all over the world, engineers, inventors and artists have been compelled to animate wood, metal, bone and porcelain with the latest technologies of their age. (2) Recorded history tells us many of these creators were men; unrecorded history would almost certainly tell a different story. They have produced dolls and ducks, human figures and ritual practices. They have delighted and disturbed in equal parts. Sometimes it was the spectacle, sometimes it was grace. Some artefacts disappeared and others have been maintained, built and rebuilt over the centuries. And running in parallel to all this were stories that were told, again almost always by men. Stories about Pygmalion, the Golem, Pinocchio, Frankenstein's monster, Rossum's robot, Thea von Harbou's Futura and even the Terminator. Stories that gave us the vocabulary with which we have encountered each new generation of automata.

In our careers as an anthropologist and a photographer we have always sat at the intersections of culture and technology and we know the need to critically examine such histories and tell stories that reflect a multiplicity of experiences and points of view. In our shared and individual practices we think about all these pasts, presents and futures, and all the many silences and elisions. Ours is a cybernetic lens, informed by our shared interest in works' pre/histories and what we can do to better inform questions we might ask of the world around us. Unpicking and unfolding these histories and stories can take you around the world. Where might one start in the case of Wolfson's *Body Sculpture*?

You could start at Artuklu Palace, in the twelfth century, near Diyarbakır in present-day Türkiye. There you would find Badī az-Zaman Abu I-ʿIzz ibn Ismāʿīl ibn ar-Razāz al-Jazarī, the palace's engineer, hard at work. (3) Building on the treatise written by the Nabu Mūsās, three scholar brothers who in the ninth century had advanced the harnessing of hydraulic power to drive machinery (4), al-Jazarī created many devices. In the palace, you might have been served mint tea by his mechanical beverage server or washed your hands before *salah* (prayers) by means of his giant metal peacock, beak open, pouring water, and if you were lucky you might have been entertained by the four automata of his musical band floating in the palace lake. The contrast of the sacred and profane: did it ever unsettle, one wonders, or just delight?

At the behest of his ruler, al-Jazarī catalogued his own work in 1206 in the exquisite *Book of knowledge of ingenious mechanical devices*. (5) It would have been clear that you were encountering a man profoundly engaged with science as well as spectacle; al-Jazarī is credited with the invention of the camshaft and a range of other mechanisms that helped control the speed and rotation of cogs and cams and several forms of early hydraulics. (6) Over the centuries, scholars and engineers have attempted to reconstruct al-Jazarī's inventions—a replica of his water clock is in the London Science Museum and his massive elephant clock is on display in the Ibn Battuta Mall in Dubai.

Or you might start in Japan. There in the late 1600s a showman by the name of Takeda Omi entertained crowds with automata called *karakuri*; the spectacle moved from the court to the Osaka streets. (7) Reverse-engineered French carriage clocks met whalebone springs to bring to life traditional Japanese puppetry: dancing children, jumping fish, public urination and poetry writing. Perhaps the most famous of these *karakuri* is the teacup automaton. This small figurine would carry a cup of tea across a table, bow on its delivery and retire again. It was described in 1675 by one onlooker: 'when given a cup of tea and pointed toward someone, in the way it moves its eyes, mouth and legs, and holds out its hands and bends its body, it looks just like a human'. (8)

Here of course the simulacrum is not just its human appearance but its human capacity. After all, in Japan the service of tea enacts a very particular piece of cultural work. This deliberate choice serves to make this *karakuri* perform a human act. Takeda's work and that of others is preserved in Hosokawa Hanzo Yorinao's three-volume manual from 1796, *Karakuri zui* or *Illustrated compendium of automata*. (9) This work, printed from wood blocks, has enabled the many attempts over the last two centuries to reanimate the teacup *karakuri* for wealthy patrons, museums and the general public.

In the United States it is not royal courts or the sideshow that compel automata; it is the market. Thomas Edison, the serial inventor and entrepreneur, briefly tinkered with automata in 1890. Edison modified and miniaturised phonographic equipment, encasing it in cloth and porcelain and creating a doll that sang. It retailed for $12. The doll was a commercial failure at the time, yet it points to our enduring fascination with the elisions of human form and emerging technologies in varied places and over many centuries. You can still find it on the internet singing its nursery rhymes, which are recognisable over 130 years later and as disturbing as they are remarkable.

Some work by the Australian poet, ballad writer and journalist Banjo Paterson reveals similar fascinations. His story 'The cast-iron canvasser' appeared in *The Bulletin* on 19 December 1891 and spins a very particular kind of Australian yarn about a failing publishing house and their attempt to automate subscription sales in the bush. Paterson's answer is the Genius, a mechanical man with a wax face and a well-sprung head and body:

> And he's dog-proof, too. His legs are padded with tar and oakum, and if a dog bites a bit out of him, it will take that dog weeks to pick his teeth clean. Never bite anybody again, that dog won't. And he'll talk, talk, talk, like a suffragist gone mad; his phonograph can be charged for 100,000 words, and all you've got to do is to speak into it what you want him to say, and he'll say it. He'll go on saying it till he talks his man silly, or gets an order. (10)

What follows is a spectacle familiar to anyone who has read Mary Shelley's *Frankenstein.* The mechanised salesman runs amok, disturbing residents in the town to which it is sent; it drowns a policeman in the river while resisting arrest and disables itself in the process.

Paterson's mechanical man lives and dies in the pre/history of the term 'robot'. The Czech writer Karel Čapek coined the term in his 1920 play *R.U.R.* or *Rossumovi univerzální roboti* (*Rossum's universal robots*) about a factory owner named Rossum and his product: artificial people made from synthetic organic matter called 'robots' from *robota* or forced labour. (11) The play was a success: translated into English, it appeared in quick succession on Broadway and the West End, and in Japan and Australia as well as BBC radio and TV productions. (12)

Robots animated by fiction and by movement soon embraced opportunities afforded by electricity and relay signals. Perhaps best known is Elektro, a walking, talking, cigarette-smoking polished-aluminium robot that was among the creations of the Domestic Appliances division of Westinghouse, the US manufacturer that routinely cannibalised components from their household irons, fridges and stoves to build their robots. (13) Elektro stepped onstage in 1939 at the New York World's Fair, dragging along its extension cord and a phone line. (14) With its wisecracks and attitude, it was an instant success and was the first time most Americans ever met a robot. An adult version was also produced and featured a striptease routine and a blushing robot face. (15) Elektro was immortalised in two very different movies: an early Westinghouse vision video, *The Middleton family at the New York World's Fair* (1939), where it plays itself, and Allied Artists' 1960 feature *Sex kittens go to college*, where it played the robot Sam Thinko. Elektro still echoes today in Hollywood's many humanoid robots and in the myriad animatronic creatures that fill Disney's theme parks. (16)

While the 1939 World's Fair introduced machines of wonder, elsewhere machines of war and defence were about to shape and determine the Second World War. In the immediate postwar period in the United States, the mathematician

Norbert Wiener was motivated to create hopeful futures and introduced the term 'cybernetics' to help define a new concept of communicating with and controlling machines. Wiener sought inspiration from the Greek word for helmsman, *kybernetes*, and was interested in how systems, be they mechanical or biological, behaved when shaped by feedback. His theory was tested through application and has informed robotics, electronic computing and artificial-intelligence systems we readily recognise today.

By the 1960s robots' impact offered new forms of art production and understanding through a new set of technical possibilities and new attitudes. Behaviour, process and performance present in the cybernetic discussions translated into art practice, curation and criticism. The exhibition *Cybernetic serendipity* was mounted in London in 1968, curated by Jasia Reichardt of the Institute of Contemporary Arts (ICA). It showcased 15 next-generation kinetic artworks or what we might think of as proto-computational automata, vying for attention among hundreds of objects sourced from over 130 contributors. (17) The pieces responded to their environment, the audience and each other and made visible their feedback loops. They were cybernetic, in a word. They were also for their day quite unlike anything anyone had encountered.

Over the exhibition's 11-week run, some 60 000 visitors flowed through ICA at Nash House on The Mall. (18) Reichardt positioned the exhibition, a cacophony of moving machines, sound and lights, computer graphics, poetry and music, as dealing 'with possibilities rather than achievements, and in this sense it is prematurely optimistic'. (19)

In Reichardt's curatorial choices, she was pushing for new attitudes to understanding art, its production and the role of the spectator in co-creating the feeling and meaning of the work. (20) As they had centuries earlier with other forms of automata, the sacred and the profane played out here in the art gallery, unsettling and delighting audiences on The Mall.

In spanning the twelfth to twentieth centuries above we have visited just some moments and stories that help illuminate one of many pre/histories of Wolfson's work in our day. We hear echoes of older forms and form makers. His work, including *Body Sculpture*, resonates with a long history of the cybernetic imaginary of Wiener's 'working simulacrum of a living organism' and with the co-creation of meaning between artist and audience through utilising new and emergent technologies. It is deeply in dialogue with cybernetic approaches and with prior intersections in the melding of technology and creativity.

In it we hear histories and stories about wonder and spectacle, about power and its lines of transmission, about knowing and forgetting and rediscovery. Until recently these were histories that revelled in the artefact but dwelt far less on its reception. Adding to the complications is the fact that recorded histories we tell and retell rarely offer an explicit critique of those self-same technologies or the multiple ways in which they are deployed for control and surveillance in the hands of monarchs, priests, soldiers, national states and commercial enterprises. These histories are equally silent to Indigenous and First Nations knowledge and skills and the consequences some emergent technologies had and would continue to have on their cultures and lands. These are histories that even as they crisscross the globe are revealing women's presence too rarely except as objects and subjects of technologies and the gaze those histories impose. These parallel stories are subtly different—we do see women as makers and doers, critique as subject and consequence as a moral play. We see fear, horror, hope and even intermittent glimpses of humour.

Wolfson's work echoes its automata predecessors and the imaginaries we have long rehearsed and it also invites us to think a little differently about those self-same pasts, presents and futures, the many silences and elisions.

Distinguished Professor Genevieve Bell AO FTSE FAHA is Director, School of Cybernetics, Australian National University. Born in and raised all over Australia, Bell is a cultural anthropologist by training. She has worked for more than 25 years at the intersections of cultural practice and technology development in the United States and Australia. Her particularly interests are in the pre/histories of our socio-technical imagination and the devices that anchor them.

Bell is now the inaugural Director of the School of Cybernetics at the Australian National University, which seeks to establish cybernetics as an important tool for navigating major societal transformations through capability building, policy development and approaches to new systems that are safe, sustainable and responsible.

Associate Professor Andrew Meares is Cybernetic Futures Lead, School of Cybernetics, Australian National University. Born and raised in Gadigal Nura /

Sydney, Meares is among Australia's pre-eminent photojournalists. He worked at the *Sydney Morning Herald* (1991–2017), where he led industry transformation in print and online. His coverage ranges from politics and portraits to bushfires, coups and war zones. He received a Walkley Award for Best Online Journalism in 2010 and has held roles as Federal Parliamentary Press Gallery President and as a political staffer.

Meares is an Associate Professor in the School of Cybernetics at the Australian National University, where he is working on how we can build futures through applied cybernetics. He curated the exhibition *Australian Cybernetic: a point through time* in 2022 and manages the school's Cybernetic Imaginations residency program.

Notes

(1) Norbert Wiener, *Cybernetics, or control and communication in the animal and machine*, Technology Press of MIT, Cambridge, MA, 1948, p 39.

(2) Much has been written on this topic. A selection includes: Ahmad Y Al-Hassan and Donald R Hill, *Islamic technology: an illustrated history*, Cambridge University Press/UNESCO, Cambridge, 1986; Christian Bailly, *Automata: the golden age, 1848–1914*, Sotheby's Publications, London, 1987, pp 12–23; Genevieve Bell, 'Making life: a brief history of human-robot interaction', *Consumption Markets & Culture*, vol 21, issue 1, 2008, pp 22–41; Donald R Hill, *A history of engineering in classical and medieval times*, Croom Helm, London, and Open Court, La Salle, 1984; Adrienne Mayor, *Gods and robots: myths, machines, and ancient dreams of technology*, Princeton University Press, Princeton, 2018; Frederik Schodt, *Inside the robot kingdom: Japan, mechatronics, and the coming robotopia*, Kodansha International, Tokyo, 1988; ER Truitt, *Medieval robots: mechanism, magic, nature, and art*, University of Pennsylvania Press, Philadelphia, 2015; Gaby Wood, *Edison's Eve: a magical history of the quest for mechanical life*, Anchor Books, New York, 2002.

(3) Ibn al-Razzaz al-Jazari, *The book of knowledge of ingenious mechanical devices*, trans Donald R Hill, D Reidel, Dordrecht, 1974, p 3.

(4) Banu (sons of) Musa bin Shakir, *The book of ingenious devices*, trans Donald R Hill, D Reidel, Dordrecht, 1979.

(5) Ibn al-Razzaz al-Jazari, p 15.

(6) Hill, 1984, pp 146–52.

(7) Schodt, pp 59–60.

(8) Sakaku Ihara quoted in Schodt, p 60.

(9) Hosokawa Hanzo Yorinao, *Karakuri zui or Illustrated compendium of automata*, Kyoto, 1796.

(10) 'The Banjo', 'The cast-iron canvasser', *The Bulletin*, vol 11, no 618, 19 December 1891, p 7; the quote used here is taken from the (revised) version published in A B Paterson, *Three elephant power, and other stories*, Angus and Robertson, Sydney, 1917, p 23.

(11) Karel Čapek, *R.U.R.*, trans Paul Selver and Nigel Playfair, Dover Publications, Mineola, 2001.

(12) Genevieve Bell, 'Smart, fast and connected: what it means to be human and Australian in the digital world', *Boyer Lectures*, episode 3, Ultimo, Australian Broadcasting Corporation, 2017, https://www.abc.net.au/radionational/programs/boyerlectures/series/2017-boyer-lectures/8869370.

(13) Scott Schaut, *Robots of Westinghouse: 1924–today*, Mansfield Memorial Museum, Mansfield, 2006, pp 91–200.

(14) Schaut, p 100.

(15) Schaut, p 182.

(16) Andrew Kiste, *Walt Disney and the 1964–1965 New York World's Fair: great moments,* Theme Park Press, New York, 2019.

(17) Reichardt described the following as cybernetic sculptures: *Cysp 1*, Nicolas Schöffer; *Metamatic*, Jean Tinguely; *Sound activated mobile*, Edward Ihnatowicz; *Albert*, John Billingsley; *Colloquy of mobiles*, Gordon Pask; *Rosa bosom (R.O.S.A. – Radio operated simulated actress)*, *Mate* and *Owl*, Bruce Lacey; *Robot K-456*, Nam June Paik; *Cybernetic sculpture*, Wen-Ying Tsai; *Entrechats II*, Frank Malina; *Hogle-Burdick chromoluxite organ*, Richard Hogle; *Scanner*, James Seawright; *Honeywell forget me not (peripheral pachyderm computer)*, Rowland Emett; *Dioximoirekinesis*, Irving Good and Martine Vite. In Jasia Reichardt, 'Cybernetic serendipity: the computer and the arts', *Studio International*, 50th anniversary edition, 1968.

(18) Jasia Reichardt, '"Cybernetic Serendipity"—getting rid of preconceptions', *Studio International,* vol 176, no 905, Nov 1968, p 176.

(19) Reichardt, 1968, p 5.

(20) Edward A Shaken, 'Cybernetics and art: cultural convergence in the 1960s', in Bruce Clarke and Linda Dalrymple Henderson, eds, *From energy to information*, Stanford University Press, Palo Alto, 2002, pp 155–77. Roy Ascott, 'The cybernetic stance: my process and purpose', *Leonardo*, vol 1, no 1, 1968, pp 105–12. Michael J Apter, 'Cybernetics and art', *Leonardo*, vol 2, no 3, 1969, pp 257–65.

Body Sculpture credits

Mark Setrakian, Wolfson's principal collaborator, Roboticist, Artist, Software Engineer, Choreographer, Composer and Percussionist

Operations and maintenance technicians: Ted Marchant, Senior Technician and Lead Operator; Brennan Lowe, TSE Programmer; Alison Klein, Junior Technician; Antonio Gomez-Rubio, Junior Technician; Syd Klinge, Senior Technician

Production support: Dave Emery, Stage Manager; Gregory Nicholson, Animator; Dave Barclay, Animator; Jesus Guerrero, Modeler; Todd Moyer, Fabricator

Spectral Motion: Mark Viniello, Project Supervisor; Lino Stavole, Project Supervisor; Dev Kumar, Battery Developer; Bill Phillipps, Technology Supervisor; Louie Lamble, Animatronic Technician

Concept Overdrive: Steve Rosenbluth, President; Konstantin Smola, Programmer; Thomas E. Burgess, Programmer; Jelani Felix, Programmer

MoCo FX: Glen Winchester, Director; Andrew Peacock, Machine Vision Expert

Killstress Designs: Tyler Smutz, President; Minglie Chen, CEO; Jeff Sharratt, Lead Install Technician

Poetic Kinetics: Stella Cho, Project Manager; James Peterson, Project Manager

Consultants: Eli Keszler, Composer and Percussionist; Daphne Fernberger, Choreographer; Marne van Opstal, Choreographer; Irme van Opstal, Choreographer; Stefan Haves, Comic Act Designer and Clown Expert; Lindsey Blaufarb, Choreographer; Craig Hollamon, Choreographer; Adam Linder, Choreographer

Jordan Wolfson Studios: Eva Chimento, Studio Director; Kenzy El-Mohandes, Jason Kotara, Studio Managers; Russell Barsanti, Production Manager; Chip Barrett, Studio Assistant

Gagosian: Sarah Watson, Director; Sophia Gutierrez, Assistant; Madeline Amos, Senior Registrar

National Gallery acknowledgements

The Hon Anthony Albanese MP, Prime Minister of Australia

Governing Ministers: The Hon Tony Burke MP, Minister for the Arts; Susan Templeman MP, Special Envoy for the Arts

National Gallery Council: Ryan Stokes AO, Chair; Abdul-Rahman Abdullah; The Hon Richard Alston AO; Esther Anatolitis; Ilana Atlas AO; Stephen Brady AO, CVO; Helen Cook; Alison Kubler; Dr Nick Mitzevich, Director; Sally Scales; Prof Sally Smart

National Gallery Foundation: His Excellency General the Hon David Hurley AC, DSC (Retd), Patron of the National Gallery Foundation; Stephen Brady AO, CVO, Chair; Philip Bacon AO, Deputy Chair; Julian Beaumont OAM; Anthony Berg AM; Robyn Burke; Julian Burt; Terrence Campbell AO; Sue Cato AM; The Hon Ashley Dawson-Damer AM; James Erskine; Tim Fairfax AC; Andrew Gwinnett; Hiroko Gwinnett; John Hindmarsh AM; Wayne Kratzmann AM; The Hon Dr Andrew Lu AM; Dr Peter Lundy RFD, Secretary; Michael Maher; Dr Michael Martin; Dr Nick Mitzevich, Director; Roslyn Packer AC; Penelope Seidler AM; Ezekiel Solomon AM; Kerry Stokes AC; Ryan Stokes AO; Ray Wilson OAM

National Gallery Executive: Dr Nick Mitzevich, Director; Susie Barr, Assistant Director, Marketing, Communications and Visitor Experience; Natasha Bullock, Assistant Director, Collections and Exhibitions; Sophie Gray, Project Director, Capital Works Taskforce; Alison Halpin, Chief Operating Officer; Bruce Johnson McLean, Wierdi/Birri-Gubba peoples, Assistant Director, First Nations Engagement, Head Curator, First Nations Art; Adam Lindsay, Projects Director; Felicity McGinnes, Chief Finance Officer; Heather Whitely Robertson, Assistant Director, Learning and Digital; Helen Gee, Sophie Hunter, Jennifer Barrett, Brittany Burgess, Zoe Bennett, Sam Somers and Ana Balta, Directorate

Curatorial Team: Russell Storer, Head Curator, International Art

First Nations Engagement Team: Bruce Johnson McLean, Wierdi/Birri-Gubba peoples, Assistant Director, First Nations Engagement, Head Curator, First Nations Art; Cara Kirkwood, Mandandanji/Mithaka peoples, Head of First Nations Engagement and Strategy; Georgia Mokak, Djugun people, Senior Coordinator, First Nations Partnerships and Strategy

National Gallery Project Team: Natalie Beattie, Head of Registration, and staff; Samantha Braniff, Head of Partnerships, and staff; Jade Carson, Chief Information Officer, and staff; Georgia Close, Head of National Learning, and staff; Sam Cooper, A/Head of Digital, and staff; Tracy Cooper-Lavery, Head of Sharing the National Collection, and staff; Ben Donaldson, Head of Capital Works Taskforce, and staff; Terri Dwyer, Head of Human Resources, and staff; Mary Fisher, Head of Financial Accounting, and staff; Stefan Giammarco, Head of Visitor Experience, and staff; Deborah Hart, Head Curator, Australian Art, and staff; Shireen Huda, Head of Governance and Strategic Planning, and staff; Greg Ible, Head of Estate Management, and staff; Cara Kirkwood, Mandandanji/Mithaka peoples, Head of First Nations Engagement and Strategy, and staff; Elizabeth Little, Manager Research Library and Archives, and staff; Marika Lucas-Edwards, Principal Content Strategist, and staff; Elizabeth Malone, Head of Commercial Operations, and staff; Laura McElhinney, Head of Financial Planning and Analysis, and staff; Fiona McQueenie, Head of Communications, and staff; Dominique Nagy, Head of Exhibitions, and staff; Kanesan Nathan, Head of Marketing, and staff; Mary-Lou Nugent, Manager Touring Exhibitions, and staff; Russell Storer, Head Curator, International Art, and staff; Maryanne Voyazis, Head of Development and Executive Director, National Gallery Foundation, and staff; Debbie Ward, Head of Conservation, and staff; Daryl West-Moore, Head of Creative Studio, and staff; Jan Wojna, Head of Project Management Office, and staff

Curator's acknowledgements

Thank you to Jordan Wolfson for leading us on this extraordinary journey. I express my gratitude to his tireless studio team, particularly his robotics collaborator Mark Setrakian and the current and former Studio Directors, Eva Chimento and Kenzy El-Mohandes. Sincere thanks also go to the Los Angeles production team, including James Peterson and Stella Cho at Poetic Kinetics, Tyler Smutz, Minglie Chen and Jeff Sharratt at Killstress Designs, Steve Rosenbluth, Thomas E Burgess and Jelani Felix at Concept Overdrive, Glen Winchester at MoCo FX, Ted Marchant, Brennan Low and Alison Klein.

I would also like to extend special thanks to Sadie Coles and Matt Glenn, Sarah Watson at Gagosian, and Alex Tuttle and Linda Yun at David Zwirner Gallery for their generous support. I am grateful for the research and technical support of the ANU School of Cybernetics, including Professor Genevieve Bell, Andrew Meares, Zhu Xuanying and Mina Henein.

Deep thanks go to the numerous current and former National Gallery staff who have been involved throughout the long development of this project. Jaklyn Babington and Shaune Lakin provided curatorial oversight at different phases of the project, with support from Vy Tsan and Peter Johnson. The project management has been skilfully steered by Sally Brand, Jan Wojna and Jane Wild, and the exhibition installation and design has been expertly managed by Dominique Nagy, Daryl West-Moore and Emma Doy. Conservators Sarah McHugh, Alysha Redston and Lisa Addison and registrars Bruce Egan and Georgia Cunningham ensured that the work arrived in Australia safely and securely, while lighting and technical support has been ably provided by Taron Scholte, Kieran Maher, Marcus Hayman, Mark Mandy, Adam Clarkson, Jessica Smith, Jade Carson and Greg Ible.

I would like to thank National Gallery of Australia Director Nick Mitzevich for his vision and dedication to this project. Sincere thanks also go to Heather Whitely Robertson and the Learning and Digital teams, and to Susie Barr and the Marketing, Communications and Visitor Experience teams for their contribution in shaping the engagement, programming and promotion of the exhibition, and to Penny Sanderson and Meagan Down for overseeing this publication.

Russell Storer

Jordan Wolfson
United States of America
born 1980
Body Sculpture 2023
mixed media
overall dimensions 429 × 1798 × 1100 cm (h × w × d)
edition 1 of 3 with 2 APs
Purchased 2019
2019.706
© Jordan Wolfson, 2023
Image folio: *Body Sculpture*, photographer, David Sims, 2023; Jordan Wolfson, School photo, 1985
All photographs courtesy the artist

Title: *Body Sculpture*: Jordan Wolfson
Editor: Russell Storer
ISBN: 978 0 642 33503 6
First published: December 2023
Book design: Joseph Logan and Jordan Wolfson, assisted by Anamaria Morris
Text editor: Alan Lockwood
Proofreader: Robert Nichols
Rights and permissions: Ellie Misios and Monica Tran, National Gallery of Australia
Assistant Publishing Manager: Meagan Down, National Gallery of Australia
Publishing Manager: Penny Sanderson, National Gallery of Australia
Pre-press: Altaimage New York
Printed by: Adams Print

Body Sculpture Jordan Wolfson